WILDLIFE SURVIVAL

Polar Bears
in DANGER

by Helen Orme

Consultant: Downs Matthews, Director Emeritus
Polar Bears International

BEARPORT
PUBLISHING

New York, New York

Credits
t=top, b=bottom, c=center, l=left, r=right
Alamy: OFC, 6, 9, 10-11, 12, 14–15, 16–17, 18l, 18–19, 20–21, 23, 25, 27t.
Corbis: 5, 13, 27b, 28, 29, 31, 32.
Every effort has been made to trace the copyright holders, and we apologize in advance for any unintentional omissions. We would be pleased to insert the appropriate acknowledgments in any subsequent edition of this publication.

Library of Congress Cataloging-in-Publication Data

Orme, Helen.
  Polar bears in danger / by Helen Orme.
    p. cm. — (Wildlife survival)
  Includes index.
  ISBN-13: 978-1-59716-264-7 (library binding)
  ISBN-10: 1-59716-264-7 (library binding)
  ISBN-13: 978-1-59716-292-0 (pbk.)
  ISBN-10: 1-59716-292-2 (pbk.)
  1. Polar bear—Juvenile literature. I. Title. II. Series.

  QL737.C27O76 2007
  599.786—dc22
                          2006012526

For more information, write to Bearport Publishing Company, Inc., 101 Fifth Avenue, Suite 6R, New York, New York 10003. Printed in the United States of America.

10 9 8 7 6 5 4 3 2 1

The Wildlife Survival series was originally developed by ticktock Media Ltd.

Table of Contents

Life in the Arctic 4

Mothers and Cubs .6

Leaving the Den 8

Life in the Sea 10

Finding Food 12

Hunting Polar Bears 14

A New Danger 16

Coming to Town .18

Studying Polar Bears 20

A Difficult Future .22

Just the Facts 24

How to Help 30

Glossary 31

Index 32

Life in the Arctic

The **Arctic** is home to the polar bear, the world's biggest land **predator**. In the Arctic Circle, a large part of the sea remains frozen all year. This area is called the ice cap. In winter, the sea around the ice cap freezes, too. Polar bears spend the fall, winter, and spring hunting on the frozen sea.

Arctic Circle

icy sea

ice cap

In the winter, the Arctic gets extremely cold. Temperatures can go as low as -50°F (-45°C).

Mothers and Cubs

In early winter, the female polar bear builds an underground **den** in a snowbank. Her cubs will be born there.

The family lives in the den until spring. The cubs feed on their mother's milk. The mother doesn't hunt for food. She doesn't need to eat. She is able to live off her body fat.

A polar bear's den is about three feet (1 m) high and six feet (2 m) long. It has a narrow hole to let in air.

Leaving the Den

In early April, the family leaves the den so that the mother can hunt for food. If she doesn't get anything to eat, her cubs cannot survive. They depend on her for food.

The mother must guard her babies carefully after leaving the den. Hungry predators, such as wolves and adult male polar bears, hunt bear cubs to eat.

For two weeks after the cubs are born, polar bear families stay close to the den entrance.

 Inside the den, the temperature can be 40°F (4°C) warmer than outside.

Life in the Sea

Polar bears are strong swimmers. They spend a lot of time in the sea. They swim from **ice floe** to ice floe, hunting for seals.

Polar bears' bodies are perfect for the water. The bears use their **webbed** feet as paddles. Their thick, oily fur keeps them warm in the icy sea.

Polar bear cubs
quickly learn to swim.
If they become tired,
they ride on their
mother's back.

Finding Food

Polar bears eat seals. To hunt them, a bear waits at an ice hole. When a seal comes up from underwater to breathe, the polar bear pounces. The bear kills the seal by hitting it with its paw.

Polar bears spend more than half of their day hunting. However, they may catch only one seal every four to five days.

Adult polar bears mainly eat seal **blubber**. The seal meat is eaten by young bears and other animals, such as Arctic foxes.

A baby seal

Hunting Polar Bears

For 1,000 years, the **Inuit people** of Northern Canada have hunted polar bears for their meat and fur. When other hunters from around the world began killing these animals for sport, the number of polar bears went down. So the government passed laws to limit the killing of polar bears. Also, anyone who wants to hunt them needs to get a license.

About 700 polar bears are legally hunted and killed each year.

A New Danger

Today, polar bears face a new danger—**global warming**. Polar bears need the floating sea ice to hunt. Yet each year global warming causes the sea ice to melt earlier and freeze later than in previous years. When there is no ice in the spring or fall, the bears can hunt only in the winter.

Without ice, it is also difficult for young polar bears to travel. They cannot swim the long distances between ice floes.

Adult polar bears can swim long distances without stopping. Some have gone more than 60 miles (97 km) without a rest.

Coming to Town

Sometimes hungry polar bears come into the towns of Northern Canada looking for food. Polar bears will not usually kill people, but they can be dangerous. People in the towns need to be protected.

If polar bears do turn up, special hunters shoot the animals with a dart gun, putting them to sleep. The bears are then taken to a safe place by helicopter.

Polar bears are big eaters. One bear can eat up to 100 pounds (45 kg) of blubber at one meal.

These bears are searching for food in a garbage dump.

Studying Polar Bears

After a bear has been hit by a dart and falls asleep, scientists can then examine the animal. They can figure out whether or not the bear is healthy and how much it weighs. If the animal has lost weight, it may mean that food is getting harder to find.

Some polar bears are fitted with radio collars that send signals to a **satellite.** The collars allow scientists to track polar bears.

A Difficult Future

Life has become very difficult for polar bears. Global warming is damaging their **habitat**. Drilling for oil and mining is causing **pollution** and changing the bears' **environment**.

However, much is being done to save polar bears. Scientists now know more about them. Fewer people are hunting them while more people are protecting these animals. Polar bears can survive in the future, but they will continue to need human help.

No one knows exactly how many polar bears are alive today. The best guess is between 25,000 and 40,000.

In this picture, a special bus allows scientists and tourists to study and watch polar bears.

Where Do Polar Bears Live?

- Polar bears live in the icy Arctic areas of Alaska, Canada, Greenland, Norway, and Russia.

- The Arctic Circle is the most northern part of Earth. It is full of life. The sea has plenty of fish, whales, and seals. In the summer, small, tough plants grow on the **tundra.**

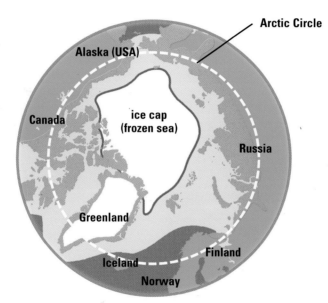

The colors on this map show what happens in the Arctic Circle throughout the year.

☐ Sea that is always frozen

■ Sea that does not freeze in winter

■ Sea that freezes in winter and breaks up into drifting ice in summer

■ Land that is covered with ice and snow in winter

More About Polar Bear Bodies

- Polar bears have two layers of fur to keep them warm and dry. They are so good at staying warm that they sometimes get too hot. The bears cool off by swimming or eating snow.

- Polar bears lose very little heat because they have small ears and noses.

- A polar bear's paws measure about 12 inches (30 cm) across. They are webbed for swimming and have hair on the bottoms to grip the ice.

Male
Weight: up to 1,323 pounds (600 kg)
Height: 10 feet (3 m)

Female
Weight: up to 772 pounds (350 kg)
Height: 7 feet (2 m)

More About Polar Bear Food

- Besides seals, polar bears also hunt small whales, dolphins, and walruses.

- If meat is hard to find, polar bears will eat berries or plants.

- Polar bears rely on their great sense of smell to hunt. They can smell food from 20 miles (32 km) away.

Arctic Food Web

This food web shows how animals in the Arctic depend on plants and other animals for food. The arrows in the web mean "are food for."

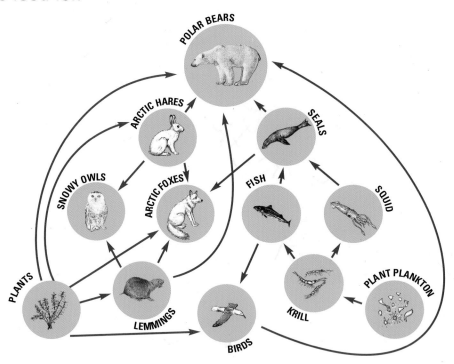

More About Family Life

- Female polar bears give birth during the months of January and February.

- When they are born, cubs are very small. They weigh about 1 pound (500 grams) and are about 1 foot (30 cm) long.

- Cubs stay in the den until they are about 3 months old.

- Cubs stay with their mother and drink her milk for about 3 years.

- Most polar bear families stay together for about 4 years. Then the young bears go off on their own.

- Polar bears do not **hibernate.**

- Few polar bears live longer than 18 years in the wild.

A polar bear lies down on the snow to keep cool.

More About Polar Bears in Danger

- Though laws help control the hunting of polar bears, **poaching** is still very hard to stop.

- There are more people in the Arctic than ever before. Their activities sometimes destroy the polar bears' habitat.

- As people dig for oil, gas, diamonds, and metals in the Arctic, the land and water become polluted.

More About Global Warming

Global warming is the biggest threat to polar bears.

What is happening?

- The Arctic is warmer than it has been for 400 years. The higher temperatures are beginning to melt the Arctic ice. Scientists say that there might not be any ice left in the Arctic Ocean by 2080.

What causes global warming?

- Most scientists believe the warming is caused by **greenhouse gases**. These gases trap the sun's heat in the **atmosphere**. Since humans are burning so much oil and coal, there are more of these gases than ever before.

Why will this affect polar bears?

- Polar bears need the sea to stay frozen so that they can hunt seals. If the ice melts, they will have a very hard time finding food.

How to Help

Conservation is everyone's job. Here are some ways to help polar bears:

- Learn all you can about polar bears. Then teach others at school about the importance of helping them.

- Help an organization, such as Polar Bears International (PBI) (www.polarbearsinternational.org). Groups such as this one raise money to pay for conservation work. To help the PBI or another conservation group, have a yard sale. Sell old clothes, toys, and books. Then donate the money that is made to the group.

- Be a good conservationist. Visit www.worldwildlife.org/act/action.cfm for tips on how to help take care of the world.

Visit these Web sites for more information on polar bears and how to help them:

www.nationalgeographic.com/kids/creature_feature/0004/polar.html
www.panda.org/about_wwf/where_we_work/arctic/
polar_bear/about_the_bears/index.cfm
www.worldwildlife.org/polarbears/

Glossary

Arctic (ARK-tik) the area around the North Pole

atmosphere (AT-muhss-fihr) layer of gases that surrounds Earth

blubber (BLUH-bur) a layer of fat under the skin of animals, such as seals, whales, and polar bears

conservation (*kon*-sur-VAY-shuhn) the protection of wildlife, forests, and natural resources

den (DEN) an animal's home; a hidden place where an animal sleeps or has its babies

environment (en-VYE-ruhn-muhnt) the area where an animal or plant lives, and all the things, such as weather, that affect that place

global warming (GLOHB-uhl WARM-ing) the gradual heating up of Earth caused by greenhouse gases trapping heat from the sun in Earth's atmosphere

greenhouse gases (GREEN-*houss* GASS-ez) the gases caused by burning oil and coal

habitat (HAB-uh-*tat*) a place in the wild where an animal or plant lives

hibernate (HYE-bur-nate) to spend the winter in a deep sleep

ice floe (EYESS FLOH) a floating sheet of ice

Inuit people (IN-oo-it PEE-puhl) Native American people who live in the Arctic

poaching (POHCH-ing) hunting illegally on someone else's land

pollution (puh-LOO-shuhn) harmful material, such as oils, waste, and chemicals, that damage the air, water, or land

predator (PRED-uh-tur) an animal that hunts other animals for food

satellite (SAT-uh-*lite*) a spacecraft that circles Earth

tundra (TUHN-druh) cold, treeless land; the ground is always frozen just below the surface

webbed (WEBD) skin between the toes that helps with swimming

Index

Arctic 4, 24, 26, 28–29

Arctic foxes 12, 26

cubs 6, 8, 11, 27

dangers 14, 16, 22, 28–29

dens 6, 8, 27

feet 10, 25

food 6, 8, 12, 14, 18–19, 20, 26–27

food web 26

fur 10, 14, 25

global warming 16, 22, 29

helping polar bears 18, 20, 22, 30

hunting 4, 6, 8, 10, 12, 14–15, 16, 18, 22, 26, 28–29

ice cap 4, 24

Inuit people 14

male polar bears 8, 25

map 24

mining 22, 28

mother polar bears (females) 6, 8, 11, 25, 27

oil 22, 28–29

people 14, 18, 22, 28

pollution 22, 28

scientists 20, 22–23, 29

seals 10, 12–13, 24, 26, 29

swimming 10–11, 16, 25

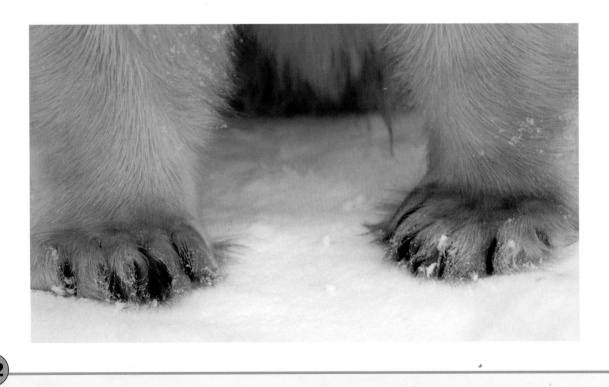